INTERROGATION

Techniques

and Tricks

to Secure

Evidence

PALADIN PRESS
BOULDER, COLORADO

$12.00

Interrogation:
Techniques and Tricks to Secure Evidence

Copyright © 1991 by Paladin Press

ISBN 0-87364-625-8
Printed in the United States of America

Published by Paladin Press, a division of
Paladin Enterprises, Inc., P.O. Box 1307,
Boulder, Colorado 80306, USA.
(303) 443-7250

Direct inquires and/or orders to the above address.

CONTENTS

Police officers generally find themselves in a quandary with respect to criminal interrogations. This is partly due to the lack of meaningful material and factual information regarding techniques of criminal interrogation.

INTRODUCTION

Unfortunately, some psychologists believe that people with high intelligence, as revealed by modern tests, are the most qualified to write or disseminate information regarding police interrogations and to solve police problems. I am inclined to disagree with this presumption.

Certainly we can learn from these eminent scholars, for psychology is the broad base for the art of interrogation. Interrogation is an art, and it is also a science. It employs psychology, physiology, and the study of human nature in general. It cannot be learned in one day, nor can it be taught in one day. There is, at present, no written and universally accepted procedure for interrogation. It is a technique that must be practiced every day if you are to become effective. The only way to learn interrogation is to actively engage in it.

So we can learn from scholars involved in the science of human behavior, but in the final analysis, what group is better qualified than the police themselves?

As far as what is most effective in the art of interrogation, our judiciary—whether in the form of judges, crown prosecutors, or defense lawyers—has not provided any meaningful information or direction with regard to this all-important phase of police science. They have left us with a list of archaic "Judge's Rules." I am of the opinion that these people are often the least qualified to judge the workings of our generation.

Police generally are not unfair in interrogations wherein they subject the suspect to unnatural stresses. We are simply exploiting those tendencies that are most common to all people. We do not go against human nature but rather along with it. To succeed, the interrogator must have confidence in himself and the technique he employs. He must have confidence in his powers of persuasion and perseverance and be able to adapt to any situation that may arise in the interrogation room.

As one author states, "The torture must come from within the suspect's own mind and not from any interrogation method employed by the police." The subject must psychologically feel that he will benefit from confessing. It is psychologically wrong to suppose that a suspect will confess for nothing. In his mind, he may believe that the very act of confessing to his crime will help him in court or be for the good of his family or the good of society. But he must, above all, believe that he is helping himself.

Our job as police interrogators in the investigation of any crime is to pave the way for the subject to confess to his crime. We must overcome any psychological or physiological barriers that prevent him from making a statement. We are simply seeking the truth in relation to the case at hand.

Attempts to change the opinions of others are as old as human speech. In recent years, civil rights groups, lawyers, and politicians alike have expressed fear that the police are manipulating the thoughts and feelings of crime suspects. Many veteran police officers are of the opinion that the courts are trying to take away the weapon of interrogation. The media has given the word "interrogation" an evil connotation. To the general public it smacks of black magic and voodoo. Subsequently, civil rights groups, lawyers, and politicians are constantly trying to handcuff us in our efforts to seek the truth.

As a result, we as professionals—and we *are* professionals—have had to broaden our base of interrogation techniques with new tactics and hidden methods. None of the techniques discussed in this book will employ physical force of any kind. They do, however, make use of a hidden battery of "hsi nao" (brainwashing) techniques to influence the emotional attitudes of the subject or suspect.

As I have already indicated, the human voice is a marvelous instrument. In the interrogation room it is one of the only instruments police officers are allowed. The power of the spoken word is fantastic, for through speech comes the power to manipulate or persuade people without having to resort to physical violence.

In the actual brainwashing techniques applied by the Chinese Communists and the Soviets, words may be supplemented by unpleasant physical treatment. But in the world of advertising, for instance, a specific brainwashing technique known as Deep Motivated Research (DMR) uses pleasing pictures, soft music, tempo music, and key phrases as weapons to sell products.

The pioneer in this field was Dr. Dichter of New York. Dichter's method was very simple. He was only reinforcing those elements of human nature that are present in all of us. For who amongst us has not been moved by a picture or the presentation of a certain type of music combined with that picture and reinforced by the voice of an announcer? In his variation of the brainwashing technique, Dichter supplemented words with pleasing pictures, soft music, and the like, which took the place of physical discomfort practiced by the Chinese Communists and Soviets.

In discussing the following techniques, I am aware that many veteran interrogators and police officers have used them without realizing what they were actually doing. A number of these techniques use ego inflation or ego deflation as their basis. The study of psychology has demonstrated that the ego may be influenced by many things, and the efficient interrogator will realize this.

Prior to entering the interrogation room, the interrogator should be in possession of all possible weapons that may help him in the interrogation. He must be familiar with every aspect of the case. He must study all reports submitted by the initial investigators, and he must check with the identification bureau for fingerprint evidence or any other evidence that may help him in the interrogation. He should also, if possible, visit the scene of the crime and familiarize himself with the crime. No soldier would go into combat without having the best weapons available, and neither should the interrogator when he enters the interrogation room.

Certainly, to begin with, we are going to do everything that is legal and right in an interrogation. We will attempt to get a confession that is free and voluntary and that may be admissible in court and will stand the test of cross examination. We will employ no tricks that could be construed as illegal. But there comes a point in many interrogations when you still do not have that statement and you know that if you go any further, your suspect's statement will be ruled inadmissible in court.

It is at this point that the interrogator must make a decision: does he leave the interrogation room without the statement, or does he proceed with other techniques which he knows will not allow the statement itself to be used but which may give him information that will lead to the securing of other evidence that may be admissible?

I suggest that at this point the Marquis of Queensbury Rules go out the window. This is where the interrogator must open up his bag of tricks and go for the recovery of the weapon, stolen property, names of accomplices, or any evidence that may be presented in court, regardless of the method employed to secure it. Given our present-day law and the rule governing the admission of evidence, one could conceivably steal evidence to be presented in court, and it could not be held out of court by the very fact that it was stolen. If we carry this through further, the interrogator could conceivably hit the suspect over the head with a baseball bat to secure evidence that will be admissible in court in the case in question.

In our careers as police officers we have heard of many weird and fantastic techniques that allegedly have been used to secure confessions. Among those referred to are the placement of a plastic bag over the subject's head, the insertion of ice cubes up the rectum, or even the application of a pair of pliers to the testicles.

I do not advocate any of the above techniques because if they were practiced, the results would be catastrophic. There is no doubt in my mind that any person subjected to such treatment would confess to anything the interrogator wanted him to. With such a technique we could find out who shot the hole in Davy Crockett's hat or who stole the Brooklyn Bridge. I'm sure that Einstein, the greatest mathematician of our time, would say that two and two makes seven if we kept hitting him over the head with a baseball bat. But again, I do not advocate violence in any form to secure a confession or statement from any suspect, no matter how heinous the crime. There is a better, more humane way, and it uses the power of the spoken word.

With that in mind, the following are some suggested techniques that have been employed successfully by many interrogators.

During war, and in peacetime for that matter, the propagandist influences his audience or country by substituting favorable or unfavorable words or names for formal names. For instance:

- "Red" for Russian or Communist
- "Union boss" for the president of a union
- "Hun," "boche," or "squarehead" for German
- "Kikes" or "Christ-Killers" for Jews

1

SUBSTITUTION

On the other hand, we have "free enterprise" for capitalism. It sounds better. In the same way, advertisers substitute long and impressive-sounding words to conceal the true identity of simple medicines or cosmetics. Otherwise, the products would not sell.

As police officers and interrogators, we must use the same technique or gimmick. We must use softer words in the place of those that will instantly conjure up in the subject's mind the seriousness of his crime. For example:

- "hurt" for "kill"
- "injure" for "stab"
- "hit" for "assault"
- "touch" or "molest" for "rape" or "indecent assault"

I'm sure that, given time, you can think of many words and phrases that can be substituted for the harsher terms commonly used to describe various crimes. By substituting words that are softer in meaning, you are minimizing the seriousness of the offense in the subject's mind.

In the field of propaganda, repetition of key words or phrases is most important. In the advertising industry, the use of slogans or key words plays an important part in whether or not a particular product will sell to the public. Some examples of repetition as well as the substitution of words in the advertising field include:

2

REPETITION

- "Compact"—used by car dealers to refer to a small car
- "Players, please"—used to promote a brand of cigarettes
- "Make the world safe for Democracy"—used by many politicians in their campaigns for election
- "A chicken in every pot"—or as our esteemed prime minister puts it, some pot for every chicken

When repeated over and over, such phrases, frequently meaningless, play a large part in advertising and politics, and they are most important in the art of interrogation.

How often we have heard the term "they say," usually followed by some statement of alleged fact; for example, "They say an apple a day keeps the doctor away."

3

APPEAL TO AUTHORITY

When using the "Appeal to Authority" technique in the field of interrogation, we must make our statement authentic, and here is where the flexibility of the interrogator and his ability to draw words and phrases out of the air is so important. For example, in the case of an indecent assault, our lines might go something like this:

"Psychiatrists say—world-famous psychiatrists say—that we are all homosexually inclined. But most of us control our sex drives. Sometimes, for one reason or another, something happens and we cannot control this drive. Ask your doctor, son, read any medical article and you will find that this is true. This act of yours is actually very natural. All we have to do is go back to ancient Greece. During the wars in Greece, each soldier had a friend that slept with him at night, and they did this every night. I certainly don't find anything so serious about it. I'm sure this happens every day in the cities of Ottawa, Toronto, New York, or wherever people gather. It's happening all the time. It's just a matter of control. Really, son, when you think of it, this has been going on in Europe for ages; we just haven't risen to that cultural level in this country."

When using this technique, the interrogator must be careful never to use any word that would indicate his true feelings about the crime under investigation. In the above case, he would avoid the use of derogatory terms such as "fag" or "faggot," "bung hole engineer," or "sword swallower." The interrogator must also avoid letting his true feelings seep through in the form of facial expressions.

To witness the power of the appeal to authority in action, you need only pick up a magazine and you are certain to find a slogan such as: "Doctors in over one thousand tests have successfully proven that Ivory Snow makes your skin look younger, softer, and lovelier than ever." Here again is the appeal to authority through the term, "doctors." Of course, the advertisers never state which doctors, and they never tell you how one tests for loveliness or softness. But the fact that doctors have proven this product can do these things gives the statement a great deal more weight in the minds of the buying public.

Again, using as an example the case of an indecent assault or any crime where sex is involved, our attempt to play down the seriousness of the crime by assuring the suspect that the rest of the world is doing it too may go something like this:

4

EVERYBODY'S DOING IT

"Son, do you think you are the only one who ever touched [substitution] a girl? I'll guarantee you that every day thousands of us as we walk down the streets think about what it would be like with a certain girl that we see. Don't think for one moment that you're the only one who has had these thoughts. Most of us simply didn't have the guts to do anything about it. Everybody does it. Girls are the same way. You don't mean to tell me that they aren't thinking of it when they see a good-looking fellow on the street. It's just human nature, that's all. This broad was probably asking for it."

This last statement leads us into the next technique, "Blame the Victim."

We can readily see that the "Everybody's Doing It" technique can lead naturally into this approach wherein we blame the victim, whether it's a child who has been sexually abused, a male or female who has been subjected to an indecent assault, or an employer who has been robbed. Our lines in a child molestation case might go something like this:

5

BLAME THE VICTIM OR EMPLOYER TECHNIQUE

"Damn it all, I can't blame you. I had a look at that kid. I'll tell you, nowadays you can't tell their age, the way they use lipstick and powder and wear these damn miniskirts. They are just asking for it, and in your case, with your old lady hot on your neck, you can't get anything at home. I don't blame you. Hell, when I spoke to this girl she even sort of looked like a prostitute to me. You just can't tell nowadays about these women. They give you the come on and then you the come on and then holler if they're caught. Hell, we're all human. We all get ideas, I don't care whether you're a policeman, a minister, or who you are. She probably only squawked because she was afraid her mother might find out. She probably led you on and then when it got right down to the business she wanted to back off. Hell, even I had ideas when I was talking to her. She's just the type that would give anybody ideas."

In the case of theft from an employer, the interrogator can ask how much the subject is earning or what type of surroundings he works in and then blame the employer:

"Hell, I don't blame you for stealing ten bucks. I probably would have taken more. Do you mean to tell me he only pays you _____ bucks a week? Who can live and support a wife and family on that kind of wage? He should be reported to the board of industrial relations. It serves him Goddamn well right. Anybody who can't afford a cash register to keep his money in deserves to lose it. Hell, anyone coming by could have put his hand in that box and taken the money. I don't blame you at all. I'll guarantee you he loses lots of money every day like this. He probably puts his hand in the till himself when nobody's looking. I'll tell you this, Mister, I'd steal too if my wife and kiddies were hungry. It takes a lot of guts to do a thing like that."

Here, I would like to digress and speak briefly about sizing up the suspect physically so that we may be better equipped to choose the proper interrogation technique. As I stated before, the effective interrogator will attempt to find out everything possible about the crime committed, but he must also find out everything possible about the suspect that he is about to interrogate. There is evidence that physique and temperament are closely related.

• Short, fat physique—these people are usually extroverts, the happy type. Eat, drink, and be merry. They tend to be susceptible to mood swings. When interrogating this type, humor them.
• Tall and slender—this type is usually with-

drawn and introverted. These are the thinkers, the scientists, the poets, the writers. They may be withdrawn, and the interrogator must attempt to bring them out by appealing to their intellect.

The interrogator must train himself to take advantage of every facet of human nature.

In dealing with a person of an obviously superior education or intellect, the interrogator must attempt to bring the suspect closer to his own level of communication. However, this technique plays upon the suspect's intellect.

6

APPEAL TO INTELLECT

Let us suppose for a moment that we were interviewing a doctor or professor from the university. We cannot hope to challenge him on his particular field of endeavor. Nevertheless, we can appeal to his intellect, and our lines may go something like this:

"Professor, by our standards in society today, you are one of the most respected people in the city of Calgary, and I just can't understand how a man of your intelligence, your intellect, could become involved in a thing like this. All my life I've always respected teachers and professors—you're, the people we learn from, you're the people we look up to. I just can't understand how a man of your caliber could become involved in a thing like this. Surely there must be a reason for it."

With this technique we do not attach any blame or even mention the act referred to. We are just appealing to his intellect to elicit a rationalization for the act.

In many instances the interrogator may be called upon to interview or interrogate a priest, a minister, or perhaps a doctor. In such cases, I have found it most beneficial to prey upon the person's position in society. For example, with a priest or a minister we might start off by trying to appeal to his religious beliefs and then slide into his position in society and the amount of respect he commands among his parishioners:

7

RESPECT FOR POSITION IN SOCIETY TECHNIQUE

"Father, I know it's hard. God in his heaven knows it's hard for a man like you. Any other man probably would have cracked up long before this. In your lifetime you have gone through many things that the ordinary man would buckle under, and God alone knows the faith that you've had to carry you through. I know the problems, the trials and tribulations that people have put on your shoulders, and yet, through all of it, you've never changed. Everyone in our town respects you; everyone in our church respects you; I respect you. I know that since this has happened there is no doubt that you have prayed to God and asked his forgiveness, just as you've taught me and others to do. Father, you've taught me that God will forgive a sin, and if there is a God in heaven—and you've taught me that there is—then he just has to forgive you for what has happened. Father, just don't let us down. We respect you. We love you. Just don't let us down. Every priest or minister that we've ever had we've looked up to. We still look up to you. I know this is going to come out all right in the end."

With this technique we keep returning to his position in society and how much he is respected. If it were a doctor we were interrogating, our appeal might go like this:

"Doctor, I know this. In your many years in practice you have become familiar with every part of the human body. You've seen death in many forms. I know it must be very hard for you because for every person who is sick and every person who dies, I would imagine it tears a little piece off you. And throughout the years you've had to steel yourself and guard against becoming too emotional, and I imagine you've come to see everybody as an organism or unit. Because if you saw them as people, individuals, I'm sure that most doctors would break. The respect you've commanded in this community and in our city is something you just can't fathom. Every one of your patients looks up to you and asks for your help. Doctor, I'm not going to be the one to pull down that reputation. You're too well respected, and if there is any way possible, any way that we can get around it, we will. There has to be a reason why this thing happened. I wish to God it had been anybody else but me that had to talk to you, because if there's one profession I do respect, it's that of being a doctor. I once wanted to be a doctor myself, but unfortunately, I didn't have the education for it."

The interrogator must be flexible. He must be

fluid and have a repertoire of words and phrases that he can draw upon at any time to fit the occasion. In the above instance, we play up the doctor's respected position in society. We build it up and then move into the next approach, the "Publicity Technique."

After having built up the person's position in society, we vaguely refer to the amount of publicity that may result if it ever became known that he was involved in this act. Our lines would probably go like this:

8

PUBLICITY
TECHNIQUE

"Doctor (Father, Professor, or in the case of a businessman, Sir), there are a lot of people, myself included, who are going to be brokenhearted over this. I only hope that there aren't too many reporters in that courtroom who know you. If it's possible, I'd like to slip you in during the afternoon when it's quiet and there aren't too many people around. What's your second name? Peter? Good. Not too many people will connect Peter Jones with Dr. Sam Jones, the eminent physician and surgeon. Doctor, the last thing I want to do is to have to bring your wife down to headquarters and interview her about this, or even speak to your kids about it. I think we can get around it somehow if we just use our heads. What happened, Doc? There must have been a reason for this. The main thing is to keep it out of the papers. Can you arrange to take holidays after this is all over, Doc?"

In this technique, we never condemn the person. And we always give him an "out," which leads into our next technique.

In this technique we supply a reason for the incident. No matter how outlandish it may be, we try to supply one so that the person confessing may save face or have some sort of justification for the offense. If a young girl is the victim of a sexual assault, for instance, our interrogation might start like this:

9

FACE-SAVING OR JUSTIFICATION TECHNIQUE

"These Goddamn kids nowadays. I don't know what the hell gets into them. They all want to try these things and then they squawk. You know, last week we had a fourteen-year-old girl; she looked like about twenty the way she was painted up. Had a miniskirt on, the whole bit, and this milkman that was delivering milk to her house got into a bit of trouble with her. There is no doubt in my mind that she was asking for it, though. Nine times out of ten they're to blame."

With this technique, the victim can serve as the ready-made excuse for the action. The interrogator can intimate in many ways that the girl kept hanging around, or that the young boy involved kept asking for money, or that the victim, no matter who it is, somehow suggested the act. When we are dealing with a robbery or a burglary, again, we can supply a reason. It could be that his wife and children are hungry, that he has been out of a job for several months, that his little girl needed a dress to go to school, that he was drunk, or that he just had a fight with his wife and didn't really understand what he was doing. The interrogator supplies the excuse for the commission of the act so that the subject may rationalize and conclude that this is an excuse for committing the act. We, as the interrogators, really do not care what reason the suspect gives for the commission of the crime so long as he admits that he did it.

This technique has proven to be most helpful in breaking down either a male or female subject charged with incest. One may wonder what possible excuse could be offered for a crime of this nature. But in the "Oedipus complex" and the Greek legend from which it got its name, we have a ready-built face-saving technique.

10

OEDIPUS TECHNIQUE

Theory has it that around the age of five years or so, the child becomes aware of other members of the family. In the male there is a more adult love for the mother, which gives rise to jealousy of the father. A girl, on the other hand, attaches herself to the father and becomes jealous of the mother. This is known among psychotherapists as the Oedipus complex.

In speaking to a male subject, we can tell him that we understand how this happened, that it is on account of the Oedipus complex, which remains dormant in every male as he grows older. Then you go on to the explanation—the legend behind the name—that follows.

Many years ago in the kingdom of Thebes, King Laius and the beautiful Queen Jocasta were married and had a son, Oedipus. At this time, the kingdom was plagued with strife and depression. It was said that the Delphic oracle had put a curse on the kingdom. This oracle had given all of the people a riddle to solve, and if it was solved, the depression, strife, and plague would be lifted.

At the same time, a rumor was circulated throughout the kingdom that the young son born to the beautiful queen was not the king's. So the king told a servant to take the child to the hills and then kill him. The servant instead left the child under a bush on the hillside to perish. However, the child was found by wandering goat herds and was taken in and cared for by the king of Corinth. When he reached his teens, he learned his fate from the Delphic oracle and fled Corinth. On his journey, he saw a beautiful golden chariot coming down the road. Afraid that it might be bandits, he threw his spear and killed the driver. Although he didn't know it at the time, he had killed his father, King Laius.

Oedipus then drove the chariot into Thebes, and all the kingdom cheered him because the king had been a tyrant, taxing them beyond endurance, throwing them into prison, and killing them for no reason whatsoever. He solved the oracle's riddle and became quite famous. In time he married the queen, who had retained much of her beauty. After the marriage ceremony, the queen found out that she had married her son and killed herself.

Once you've told the story, you can explain to the subject that the Oedipus complex exists today in every one of us. At odd times this repressed desire, this love for the mother figure if you will, pops through our superego, resulting in incest.

Sometimes you can take all of this psychological theory even further. It is said that following the Oedipus stage of a child's development, the boy usually learns the approved "masculine traits" of society from his father, and the girl learns the accepted "feminine traits" from her mother. In families where the father is deceased or absent for long periods of time, the mother becomes the stronger influence on the male child, which according to one theory, leads to homosexual tendencies. Along the same lines, should the mother be absent so that the father is the dominant figure in the family, the result is often lesbian tendencies in the female child.

Psychotherapists have also theorized that a sense of inferiority in childhood—perhaps in relation to brothers and sisters and either real or imagined—leads to a need to compensate, which sometimes is actually overcompensation. This overcompensation can also occur in children who feel inferior because of their size, and according to the same kinds of theories, can later surface in a violent nature. The child will, in effect, become a bully. Think for a moment about how many small men have become dictators: Napoleon, Mussolini, Hitler, Stalin. All of them were men of relatively small stature. Think back to your days on the beat. It was always the little guy that caused the trouble and wanted to fight.

What this indicates is that prior to the interrogation we should investigate the family tree of our suspect. Then question him about his brothers and sisters, his father and mother. Which parent is dead and how long? Which one does he like better? Are his brothers bigger? Is he the only boy in the family? Sometimes the answers will provide insight into the type of person we are dealing with and suggest the appropriate interrogation technique. The important thing is not whether the psychological theory is true or not, but whether the suspect feels that it is true. In the case of the man of small stature, for instance, does it appear that he feels he must always prove himself? If so, go along with him. Go along with human nature and suggest that perhaps he is always being picked upon by bigger people. This leads us to our next tactic, known as the "Suggestibility Technique."

Direct suggestion—aided by stage-setting—appeals to the unconscious attitudes deep within us. When caught doing something wrong, children and adults alike will attempt to rationalize their way out of the predicament. The same applies to a suspect in a crime, so it follows that we must suggest possible reasons for the commission of the crime.

11

SUGGESTIBILITY TECHNIQUE

While this technique is very similar to the "Face-Saving Technique" (page 22), the approach is slightly different. Again, we are simply suggesting a possible reason for the commission of the offense, thereby allowing the person to rationalize or escape responsibility so that he will be more likely to confess.

We may suggest the following for breaking and entering: financial difficulties, overindulgence in liquor, sickness in the family, peer pressure (e.g., he did it did it on a dare, because he was jealous).

Any one of these suggestions can be exploited as a part of the interrogation technique if the suspect shows some reaction to it. For example, if the suspect admits that he had been drinking, play upon his reduced power of recall. Does he forget things? Did he realize what he was doing? Supply the built-in suggestion that perhaps he was too drunk to really be aware that he was committing the offense—so long as you get him to admit to having committed it.

Ministers and politicians have long used the power of suggestion to persuade or motivate their audiences. John Wesley, the great evangelist, used the power of suggestion to convert people to his faith. Adolph Hitler used the power of suggestion, accompanied by music and crowds, to gain popularity and align the German people behind him. Today, evangelist Billy Graham uses props—one of them being the Bible in his right hand—as he speaks in a great emotional voice to his audience and suggests that they come to Christ and be forgiven. In the background, of course, is the beautiful sound of the organ playing, the semidarkness of the cathedral or arena, and the ever-ready assistant waiting in the aisle to help you make your commitment to Christ.

In this one, we type the suspect's name on a file, or better yet, print it with a felt marking pen in large block letters so that the subject can clearly see his name on the outside of the file. The interrogator sits in one chair and, with an indifferent attitude, pretends to be perusing the contents of this file. Sometimes a nod of the head, as though confirming what was found in the file, and an odd look at the subject will mean the difference between a confession and refusal to say anything. The main object of this approach is to cause the subject to think you have built up a conclusive file on him and have all the evidence you need.

12

FILE GIMMICK

This approach is adapted from techniques used both in religion and in brainwashing. We let the subject have a look at hell, then offer him heaven in exchange or as an alternative.

To conjure up a glimpse of hell, the interrogator might hint at the loss of a job, the loss of children's respect, perhaps the loss of a wife—and at least her condemnation. The lack of sex in prison and what a young wife might do while her husband is there can be powerful images indeed. We might point out that the suspect's wife is young and beautiful and certainly would be a target for other members of society. We can also bring up his social status and what the rest of society—and especially his neighbors—will think.

Having shown him hell, the interrogator then offers the suspect a glimpse of heaven, or a reward, as it is referred to in relation to brainwashing. We subtly imply that there will be no publicity, that there might be a way to save his job and his position in the community and prevent his neighbors from knowing about this act. The important thing is that we keep repeating the glimpse of hell and then offer him an alternative. A man who is guilty of the crime will almost certainly grab the

13

HEAVEN AND HELL TECHNIQUE (HOT AND COLD)

alternative, which, of course, is heaven.

The techniques of brainwashing involve interrogating the subject at all hours, day or night, after he has been kept in isolation and has had most of his clothes taken away. He is dressed in a sloppy pair of coveralls and a pair of shoes that are too large for him and have no shoelaces so that they flop about. He has no belt to hold up his pants. What all of this adds up to is an assault to his dignity. The fact that he has been stripped of his clothing is an attack upon his very identity. He now feels forsaken and forgotten due to the lack of familiar surroundings and the refusal of his custodians to allow him any contact at all with his loved ones or friends. He feels completely forsaken and forgotten and is at the depths of despair. It is at this point that the interrogator offers him a glimpse of heaven or a reward in the way of a cigarette, coffee, more comfortable quarters, and an opportunity to speak to his loved ones, friends, or at least another prisoner. The isolation is taken away. We can readily see how the subject begins to believe he has something to gain on the one hand and everything to lose on the other.

I am not suggesting that any police officer use the brainwashing techniques applied by the Chinese Communists or the Soviets. I do adhere, however, to the basic premise that when a subject is given a choice between heaven and hell, he will inevitably choose heaven.

Here, the interrogator puts one stick, the agent provocateur, in a cell next to the suspect's in an attempt to lure the suspect into talking about the crime in question. Agent number two is placed in another cell where he can overhear the conversation. It is most important that he just play a listening role and take no part in the actual conversation with the suspect, as handled by agent number one. If the suspect does talk to agent number one, it is possible that agent number two's testimony relating to what he overheard could be admitted as evidence in court. At the very least, the information that agent number two hears can be passed on to the interrogator and be used as a weapon in any interrogation that follows.

14

DOUBLE STICK (AGENT PROVOCATEUR) TECHNIQUE

A related point: the interrogator must remember to keep accomplices in a crime separated so they cannot lay down a story and get together on an alibi.

This approach may be initiated as follows:

"Son, if you are as innocent as you say, why waste money (do not refer to lawyer). But Son, I'm going to tell you something. If you are guilty, you get a lawyer, and make sure you get a good one because you're going to need one. There is only one person that can help you. It is not your mother; it is not your father. It is not even a lawyer or a priest or a minister, but rather you yourself. You and you alone have to make the decision. I can't help you. No priest, minister, or lawyer can help you. You've got to admit to yourself that you did it and then see your doctor and tell him the truth, or he can't help you. You've got to admit to yourself that you did do this thing, and then you've come a long way. You've made that first big step, and the rest is easy. If you can admit it yourself, you're over the first big hurdle, and you're on the way to recovery. For heaven's sake, when you see your doctor, tell him the truth. Don't you think that's good advice, Son? By the way, who is your doctor?"

The longer the suspect lets the interrogator talk without interruption, the more certain the interrogator can be that the suspect is the guilty person. In this technique, it is essential that the interrogator be

15

LAWYER GIMMICK

fluid and keep the conversation flowing without
interruption.

In any interview, the interrogator must be in complete control of the situation. If the suspect is allowed to take over, the interrogator will be forced to assume the defensive attitude. It must be the other way around.

16

CONTROL
TECHNIQUE

To begin with, tell the suspect where to sit, to refrain from smoking, and so on. This helps establish your authority over the subject. Be careful, however, that your tone of voice cannot be construed as threatening.

As long as the interrogator remains in control of the interview he can steer it down the path that he would have it take. The subject may be inclined to ramble, and through suggestive questioning you must steer the interview back into the channels you would have it take. At no time do you allow the suspect to have control of the interview.

The basic premise of this technique is that if the interrogator enlarges upon the seriousness of the crime or the number of offenses, the suspect will become rattled and confess to the one crime he is charged with in trying to deny the others that he is being blamed for unjustly. In a simple theft, for instance, an interrogator might suggest that a gun or knife was used. Of course, that makes it an armed robbery or a robbery with assault. The object is to get the subject to say, "I didn't have a gun," and thereby fall into your trap. (A similar ploy is used in the "Kiting Technique" on page 56, wherein the amount stolen is raised to what might appear incredible to the suspect.)

When the interrogator has suggested that either a gun, knife, or some other weapon has been used, it is most helpful to move into the next technique with a remark like, "I hope you stashed the gun in a safe place." This is a direct appeal to the suspect's intelligence (or conscience).

17

EXAGGERATION TECHNIQUE

This technique flows naturally from the "Exaggeration Technique." In the event that, for instance, nitroglycerine (commonly known as grease) was used in the crime, we tell the subject that we hope the grease or nitro has been stashed well because we don't want someone's arm blown off. It could be his son or his daughter, which would appeal to the conscience of the subject, a closely related technique. If it was a gun that was used in the crime, for instance, your approach might go something like this:

18

APPEAL TO INTELLIGENCE (OR CONSCIENCE) TECHNIQUE

"You've got kids of your own, and I'm damn sure you wouldn't want your kid to find it and point it at another kid or hurt himself with it. These kids nowadays can find things in funny places. I hope you put it in the river or really stashed it well. Did you stash it okay?"

Of course, the confirmation by the subject that the weapon has been stashed and there is no danger of anyone finding it is all the interrogator needs to hear in this instance. Now he knows he is on the right path and that he indeed has the guilty party. All you are worried about is that some innocent child does not find the gun, the nitroglycerine, or whatever. In this technique, the interrogator stays away from the actual crime committed and implies that he is only interested in the grease.

It is important that the interrogator find a way to establish some sort of rapport with his subject. I have found this technique most helpful. When you enter the interrogation room, your conversation should follow these lines:

19

RELATIVE TECHNIQUE

"What did you say your last name was? Black. George Black. You know, when I walked in that door I thought it was my young cousin Ralph. You look exactly like him. I can't get over the resemblance between the two of you. You're the spitting image of him. What was your mother's maiden name?"

Keep insinuating by the subtle use of questions that perhaps this man is distantly related to you. During your conversation with him, intentionally make a mistake and call him Ralph, the name of your cousin. Again, refer to the resemblance. The suspect might infer that the reason you are talking to him for this length of time is because of his resemblance to your cousin. The next step, of course, is to say that your younger cousin had exactly the same hang-up of exposing himself, but thank God we got it in time. Then you slide into the gimmick of suggesting that your younger cousin admitted to himself that he had done it, which was the first big step, and was referred to a prominent doctor for treatment. Now, of course, the younger cousin has a good job, is married, and everything is okay. The first step he had to take was to admit to himself that he had made a mistake.

While we've demonstrated how this technique can be used effectively with a crime involving sex, it may also be used for the commission of any other crime, whether it be shoplifting, narcotics, robbery, or burglary.

This technique is an attempt by the interrogator to inflate the ego of his subject. It is more effective on subjects who are prone to flattery. However, all of us can be or have been manipulated by a friend, lover, or employer. Those of us who have been married have probably been subjected to this ego inflation technique by our spouses since the very first day of our marriage! There are very few people who cannot be manipulated through the use of flattery.

20

FLATTERY
TECHNIQUE

The con artist or snowman thrives on using this technique to achieve his desired results. One need only think back on a fraud case where the accused, by the use of flattery, was able to pass worthless checks, sell worthless stocks, or obtain merchandise using nothing more than his personality and ego inflation. When questioning the witness, we were probably faced with a remark such as, "It couldn't have been him. He was such a nice man and had personality plus."

The flattery technique can be used in nearly every interrogation, except perhaps those involving violence. And even then, especially if the subject is what might be termed an ego maniac, we might still apply it. It is most effective in cases involving fraud, counterfeiting, safe cracking, breaking and entering, or shoplifting. The basic idea is to flatter the subject by using such phrases as, "Boy was that ever a clean job. It was really a neat job. We've never seen anything like this before. It must have taken a lot of planning. It was sure an expert job. I don't know how guys like you do it. You must have a lot of guts. It must have taken a long time to drill that safe. It was just as neat a job as I have ever seen."

When referring to counterfeit money or checks, play upon their authenticity. Again, intimate that a lot of time and planning must have gone into the caper, that the suspect must have used an expert engraver or some new type of process, that they look so legitimate that even you, with your years of experience, could hardly tell them from the real thing.

Quite often the interrogator will have as a subject an employee who is involved in theft or embezzlement. Generally this type of person has been subjected to office management discipline. He is not

21

WHITE COLLAR
TECHNIQUE

the "criminal type" as we in law enforcement know it, and he will respond to what might be termed ethical principles and moral standards.

The emotional approach has also proven most beneficial with the "White Collar Technique." Sometimes, the mere pat on the shoulder by the interrogator or the shaking of his hand is all that is needed to start the flow of conversation. As in any interrogation, you must delve into the background of the subject, seeking some small detail that might indicate what type of approach is warranted. The contents of the suspect's wallet may prove a gold mine. A picture of the suspect

with his young son in his arms or with his arms around his wife may be all you need. You would then question him on his thoughts about his son and wife, and in turn use those very sentiments against him.

This technique is as old as time. I'm sure that at one time or another every police officer and his partner have used this technique successfully on a suspect, no matter what crime he was suspected of.

This is a team approach and must be well thought out beforehand. The interrogators must know the type of crime committed and the background of the suspect. More importantly, from their "sizing up procedure," they should have determined that the suspect is likely to respond to this type of approach.

The bigger of the partners will assume the role of the hard-nosed detective. He is the one that becomes impatient with the suspect and his lies, starts to bang the table, talks very loud, and presses his Adam's apple against his collar to make his face become flushed so he appears to be mad. His lines may go something like this:

22

MUTT AND JEFF TECHNIQUE (HARD AND SOFT APPROACH)

"This S.O.B. is lying. He's been lying the whole time. I don't know why the hell you spend so much time with him. Why don't we just throw his ass in the bucket? I'm not going to sit here and listen to his Goddamn lies! We don't need his statement anyhow. I'm finished with him. You do what you want, but I'm getting out of here. I can't stand this S.O.B."

When this partner leaves, the remaining partner uses the soft approach:

"I don't know why he does that. He's gotten us in more trouble by getting mad and swearing than you'll ever know. Some guys are like that. Personally, I can't stand the big S.O.B. I wish to Christ I had a different partner. For God's sake, don't get him mad at you. He's a miserable S.O.B. And of course, he's my senior and can make it a little tough for me. Listen, come here a minute. (The interrogator then moves his chair closer to the suspect and assumes a conspiratorial tone whereby he drops his voice to a low level.) Look Mac, if you did it, for Christ's sake, say so before he comes back in, and I'll see what I can do. I'll put in the report. I don't want him putting in the report because he'll make it worse than it really is. Just remember, when he walks in that door, that's it, we're finished. It's the end, because he won't let me come back and talk to you. He's just that type."

What has actually happened here is that the hard-nosed detective has upset the suspect, knocking him off balance mentally. Now, while the suspect is in this state of imbalance and is more prone to the soft technique, the soft-spoken detective takes over in the exact opposite tone.

n this approach, the interrogator separates two suspects. They are usually, if at all possible, placed in the same corridor with three or four cells between them so that they cannot contact or converse with one another. After a period of time the interrogator goes to suspect number one, takes him out of the cell, and walks by number two's cell. The interrogator then lets suspect number one sit in the interrogation room for about half an hour. He does not even speak to him, he just leaves him sitting by himself in the interrogation room and then takes him back to his cell. As he is passing by the cell of suspect number two, in a voice loud enough for number two to hear, he remarks, "Thanks, George, I think that has cleared it up, and I'll see what I can do." He then places suspect number one in his cell and leaves.

23

FALSE STATEMENT TECHNIQUE (BLUFF ON A SPLIT PAIR)

One can imagine what is going on in the mind of suspect number two, especially after hearing a remark like "Thanks, George." It might go something like this: "Thanks for what? That fink—what in hell did he tell those guys? Did he fink out?"

The interrogator waits about five or ten minutes after returning number one to his cell, then comes back and gets number two and says to him in a loud voice, "It's your turn now, Jim."

In this technique we again have the suspects separated. Number one suspect is in an interrogation room, and number two is close by. He can hear the voice of the interrogator but cannot distinguish what is being said. After a period of time, the interrogator leans out of the interrogation room and yells for Bev, the secretary. He asks her in a loud voice—loud enough for suspect number two to hear—to bring her notepad. The secretary or stenographer comes into the interrogation room and remains long enough (in the mind of suspect number two) for number one to have made a confession. Again, this places suspicion in the mind of suspect number two, breaking down his will to resist the interrogator's attempts to bring about a confession.

24

SECRETARY TECHNIQUE (SETUP)

In most instances, whether guilty or not, suspects show signs of being nervous about being interviewed by the interrogator. But the guilty suspect will show definite behavioral symptoms whenever the interrogator asks a relevant question (i.e., one concerning the crime at hand).

25

BEHAVIORAL SYMPTOM TECHNIQUE

In this technique, the interrogator draws the suspect's attention to his behavioral symptoms, including any of the following:

- Blushing
- Fidgeting in his chair
- Evading answers
- Sweating at his hairline, underneath his nose, or at his sideburns
- Movement of his Adam's apple
- Breaking of eye contact (looking at the floor or the ceiling but never directly at the interrogator)
- Dry mouth
- General signs of nervousness

You keep referring to the behavioral symptoms of the suspect, commenting that an innocent party would not display such symptoms. You may imply that the suspect is falling apart at the seams, that he has given every indication that he is the guilty party.

Tell him he is killing himself by holding it in. The interrogator must train himself to look for these behavioral symptoms whenever a relevant question concerning the crime is asked. Sometimes these signs are very subtle; you must be alert to catch them.

In this approach, the interrogator again attempts to provide a ready-made excuse for whatever happened in the crime. It is similar to the "Face-Saving or Justification Technique" discussed on page 22. It is a well-known fact that people will attempt to think or rationalize their way out of a difficult situation. You have only to think back upon a time when you were asked by your sergeant or inspector why you did not do a certain thing. Immediately, a rationalization process went into operation. You attempted to think of any excuse that might get you out of the embarrassing situation.

26

ACCIDENT TECHNIQUE

So it is with the suspect. To secure a confession, we attempt to provide him with an excuse for what he did. It may be that the gun went off accidentally (although it hit the victim squarely between the eyes). It may be that while arguing or quarreling with the victim he tripped and the knife entered her heart (although she was cut to ribbons). Maybe the death was accidental—all the suspect meant to do was to take the victim's wallet, but he started to fight and the suspect hit him too hard, causing him to fall to the ground and strike his head. Maybe the rape victim went along with the "love-making" up to a certain point, but then she started to resist and the suspect was afraid she was going to scream and embarrass him. Here again, you blame the victim. You provide the ready-made excuse that the suspect just tried to stop her from screaming and went a little too far (even though the victim was strangled by her own silk stocking or a piece of rope). It makes no difference what excuse is offered; the suspect will grasp at any straw to rationalize his way out of a difficult situation.

Of course, we do not concern ourselves with what excuse the suspect offers, only that he admits to the crime in question.

This approach is most effective with a first offender or a juvenile. The interrogator suggests that the coat or purse was taken by mistake and then the suspect was afraid to return it for fear that the complainant would actually believe that he had stolen it.

27

MISTAKE TECHNIQUE

Imply that the suspect is a victim of circumstances that anyone could be caught in. Whether dealing with thefts from employers, break-ins, or burglaries, you may imply that the suspect got himself into debt by gambling, which anyone can do. Or you might suggest that he got into debt by over-purchasing furniture or appliances for his wife and clothing for his children. Any man would have done the same. He would not sit idly by and see his wife or children go without. We admire him, for above all, no man would allow his wife and children to go without and starve.

This technique can be employed when the interrogator has information suggesting that the object or money stolen is still available, and that there is a possibility of recovering it.

The interrogator implies that if the suspect could return the article or the money—or part of it—perhaps the victim would change his mind in regard to prosecution. Be very careful, however, not to promise that there will be no prosecution. Simply state that if the victim gets some of his money or merchandise back, he might change his mind about the whole matter.

Where it has been a theft from an employer, you can again play upon the small wage that the suspect receives. Tell him you would probably do the same thing—that ten to one the boss himself steals from the till every day and cheats on his income taxes but is never caught. Suggest that it is the employer's own fault for making his employees open to temptation by leaving cash around unsecured, and that if he gets some of it back, he might understand this and decide not to prosecute.

28

CAN YOU TAKE IT BACK TECHNIQUE

Many times, victims of a burglary will state for insurance purposes that they had more merchandise or cash stolen than what was actually taken by the thief. Interrogators can use the same ploy when questioning a suspect, always doubling the amount of money or merchandise involved. Where the amount actually stolen was one thousand dollars, for instance, we keep referring to the two thousand dollars that was stolen during the interrogation. This creates an imbalance in the mind of the suspect, leaving him with a dilemma. He does not know for sure if he will be convicted, but he reasons that if the amount of two thousand dollars is included in the report he will receive a harsher penalty. Therefore, he states he did not steal two thousand dollars but in fact only one thousand.

29

KITING
TECHNIQUE

After speaking to the suspect about his background, the interrogator eventually turns the conversation around to the subject at hand. You get him to admit that he had thought, at one time or another, about taking the article or money, about how easy it would be to break into the premises or take the money from the till. Then, through subtle questioning, get him to admit that at one time or another he may have taken a dollar or two or perhaps a small article from his place of employment. Then extend this to a period of time, asking him how much he may have taken over a period of two months. The idea is to keep extending it gradually so that you can say that he has already admitted to stealing from the company he worked for and that this is a crime in itself. You can readily see how easy it would be to jump from this admission to the present case or crime in question. The key is to start out by getting the suspect to admit that he had thought about taking the article or money in question.

30

EXTENSION TECHNIQUE

When a constable on the beat catches the suspect in the actual commission of the crime, the hot confession technique is most advantageous.

As a police officer, when you suddenly come across

31

HOT CONFESSION TECHNIQUE

the accused in the act of the crime, you may draw your pistol or revolver, not knowing what to expect in the way of retaliation by the accused. After placing the accused under arrest, with your revolver still in hand, you inform him that he no doubt is the party that has been responsible for the more than fifty burglaries or the rash of armed robberies in that particular district.

At the time of his arrest, the suspect is in a state of mental imbalance. While his resolve is weakened as a result of his present predicament, he is most liable to deny being responsible for fifty or sixty burglaries, saying that he has only done ten or twenty burglaries, or maybe just four or five armed robberies. You exert pressure by accusing the suspect of a great number of crimes in the hope that he will choose the lesser of the two evils and confess to the actual number that he did do.

This approach usually works with convicts who have records or suspects with prior records. You might go about it like this:

"Charlie, the last time you were in you didn't talk either. How long did you do, five years? You had a lot of time to think, eh Charlie. The same thing can happen this time, Charlie. Don't talk and you'll get yourself another five. You were sent away the last time, weren't you? Don't be stupid for Christ's sake, Charlie. Think, man. I credit you with more intelligence than that. What do you think you will get this time? Seven, eight, nine years? Look, nobody was hurt. Maybe if nobody squawks we can make it straight theft instead of armed robbery. Did the broad in the store see the "chunk" or "toad stabber?" If she didn't, it's just theft. We could make it straight theft. You'll be laughing, Charlie. We'll only charge you with three of these offenses, even though you've done more. We were thinking of conspiracy, and think, Charlie, you are right for the habitual charge."

32

LOGICAL APPROACH (APPEAL)

With suspects who have records, this approach has proven most helpful. This type of suspect will attempt to make the best deal possible when they are confident that the police have the goods on them.

They are afraid of the word conspiracy, and the ones with the necessary ingredients for a habitual charge will often jump at the chance to cop out for maybe three smaller ones or a charge of straight theft rather than armed robbery. When faced with the prospect of being convicted of a number of crimes, such suspects will almost certainly seek the lesser of two evils and confess to the actual number that they committed.

Here, you purposely try to deflate the suspect's ego. You must be very careful to size up the suspect. If he seems to be a screw-up who is outwardly insecure and clumsy, or if he is actually a very good thief who takes pride in his work, he is likely to be vulnerable to the following tactic:

33

ATTACK ON VANITY (EGO DEFLATION)

"You, Charlie! You creep. For Christ's sake who helps you on with your pants in the morning, your mother? Look at you, you're wearing a belt. I bet somebody has to wipe your rear end for you every time you go to the can. You couldn't do this job. You should be out on the corner selling pencils. You do this job? Impossible. You're nothing but a has-been. You can't even go to the shithouse by yourself. Knock it off, Charlie. Who planned it for you? What did you get for it, ten dollars for shining the guy's shoes?"

34

YES OR NO TECHNIQUE (LAST CHANCE APPEAL)

In this technique, the interrogator is attempting to create an imbalance in the mind of the accused. You are trying to rattle him and get across to him that, as soon as you leave the room, he does not have another chance to talk to anyone connected with the police to whom he can tell his side of the story. He just has this one chance, and he had better take advantage of it. It is his last chance, and you might inform him of that in the following way:

"Look, Mister, my time is valuable. I don't have time to jack around with a second-rater like you. I'm going to give you just one chance. All I want out of you is a yes or a no. Understand that. All I want out of you is a yes or no. Don't interrupt me. Just say yes or no. Nothing else. Start lying to me, Mister, and I'll walk right out that door and you're dead. You're dead, dead, dead. You can go upstairs and just rot. All you get is one chance because when I leave here, that's it. You don't get another chance. That's all. All I want out of you is a yes or a no and that's all."

In this technique, the interrogator drops his voice very low, and his approach may be something like this:

"Come over here, Charlie. I don't know whether this place is bugged or not but come over here so I can talk to you. Some of these guys snoop at the doorway and try to hear what is going on. For Christ's sake, if you did it, you did it, and that's all there is to it. If it was an accident, for Christ's sake, say so. Maybe we can dress it up a little. Maybe we can get you a little less time; maybe we can deal. But damn it, don't say I ever said this to you, because if you do, I'll say you are a liar and deny everything. Use your head, Charlie, you can get yourself off the hook. Don't talk too loud, just keep your voice down to a whisper, okay, Charlie?"

35

CONSPIRACY TECHNIQUE

In this technique, you reverse roles with the criminal. Ask him what he would do in your position. Your lines may go something like this:

"Look, Bill, I didn't drop in out of the sky. You know why I'm here. What would you do if you were in my place? What do you want me to do? Just give me one thing to hang my hat on. Were you drunk? What happened? Do you think you can get the stuff back? I'm asking you, what would you do in my position? I'll do anything you want me to. But give me a break; you've got to give me something to hang my hat on."

Putting the suspect in your position as the interrogator and letting him make the decision has proven very effective because the suspect will often attempt to make some deal for himself.

36

WHAT WOULD YOU DO TECHNIQUE (APPEAL)

When a suspect tells one lie, he must continue to tell lies to support his first one. In this instance, when you catch the suspect in his first lie, you purposely foster more lies. You feed him material that causes him to lie, and finally, when you have built up a pyramid of lies, you discredit the first one by exposing his other lies. Naturally, the pyramid falls down. Suppose the suspect states that he was in a certain location. We then come up with a nonexistent accident in that location and our lines may go something like this:

"You say you were on 14th Avenue and Main Street, Bill, about eleven o'clock last night? By golly, when I think of it, I recall we had a vag slip put in on you there, with your car at that! One of the constables on the beat was attending to the fire and saw you there."

What you have done here is purposely foster a lie that your suspect will go along with. When he agrees to all of this to support his first lie, he falls right into your trap. Since there was no fire and no constable on the beat at that location, and Bill's car was never seen in the area, it becomes obvious that he was not there at all.

37

PYRAMID OF LIES TECHNIQUE

You must be 90 percent sure that there was another person involved in the offense before you can use this technique. The idea is to indicate to the suspect that it's not he you suspect. He is cold. It's his accomplice you're worried about. It goes something like this:

38

THE OTHER GUY TECHNIQUE

"Look, Bill, we're not worried about you. Jesus Christ, did you know that guy with you was packing a 'chunk' on this one? He's the guy we want. He's a bad one. Last week in Edmonton he allegedly pulled another caper like this, only in that one he hit the guy over the head."

You go on talking about his partner, who was supposedly carrying a pistol or knife on this caper—which, of course, makes the offense a lot more serious in the mind of the suspect. But you still give him an out by saying that it was the other person who was carrying the gun or the knife. The object is to get the suspect to come back with the remark that he didn't realize this fellow was packing a gun or carrying a knife, and you've cut your first wedge into the interrogation.

This is an attempt to place the idea in the suspect's mind that the first person to talk is the one who will be believed. Your lines go something like this:

"Charlie, somebody always talks about a caper. It can be a witness, or it could be the guy you did it with. If that happens, you can bet your ass it's all going to fall on you, because remember this—the first guy who talks is the one that we'll believe. Get your story in first, Charlie, and you're the guy they'll believe. Do you think your partner is going to take all the blame when he is caught? Like hell he is. If the other guy talks first, you face an uphill battle all the way, Charlie, because you just don't know what he has said."

39

SOMEBODY ALWAYS TALKS TECHNIQUE

This approach is usually used on a person who belongs to the Masons, the Knights of Columbus, or any other service club that, from the contents of his wallet or some piece or jewelry, you are able to ascertain he belongs to. Your approach should be something like this:

40

SERVICE CLUB OR SOCIETY TECHNIQUE

tain he belongs to. Your approach should be something like this:

"Charlie, I want to tell you something. I notice you are wearing a Masonic ring. Charlie, not too often do we have a Mason in here. I am going to tell you this, no Mason has ever lied to me. Does that ring actually mean anything to you? By all the standards of your club, you profess to be a man, and, Charlie, a man admits his mistakes. Just remember this—we have all made mistakes, every one of us has made mistakes. Even the good Lord said, 'A just man falls seventy times seven, but he shall be forgiven.' You're supposed to be a good Mason, Charlie. Am I getting through to you, Charlie? Do you understand what I am trying to tell you? Be a man. Just remember this—your wife will respect you for being a man. She can understand that you made a mistake, but the one thing your wife and kids will never forgive you for is lying to them."

As you can see, the interrogator should be constantly on the alert for some sign of membership in a service club or fraternity, whether it be a Rotary pin, Masonic ring, or membership card. Any of these are indications that you might be able to use this technique against the suspect. Draw attention to the lofty ideals of the service club that he takes so much pride in and visits every Wednesday or Thursday night, and in this way prey upon his conscience.

In using this technique, you indicate to the suspect that the next question is a very important one and you want him to think very, very seriously before he answers it. You might say something like this:

41

I WANT YOU TO TALK TECHNIQUE

"Charlie, I want you to seriously consider this, and before you answer this question, I want you to think, man. Take your time, but remember, when I ask it, I am asking for a hell of a good reason. Recognize that. I must know something to ask this question, and remember, you are going to be stuck with the first answer you give, so just be careful and make sure you think before you speak. Just be careful—I am not asking this question for the good of my health, but it could be for the good of your health."

The key is to insinuate that you know the answer to the question but are just asking it to test his truthfulness. In other words, you suggest to the subject that you know he is going to lie. The subject, knowing this, often tells the truth without even waiting to hear what the question is.

This is another technique whereby we attempt to supply a ready-made excuse for the commission of the crime. This time it's not the victim's fault, but rather the fault of society. It might go something like this:

"Charlie, I know what a hard life you've had. Your parents were divorced; you were kicked around from pillar to post. You lived in foster homes for fifteen years. You never had the chance that other kids had. You never went to school; you never went to church; you never played games like the other kids. The only game you ever played was in reform school. It's no damn wonder that you had to turn to things like this. You didn't have the same chance as the other kids. Society has really kicked you in the ass. You've been unlucky most of your life, and today you were unlucky enough to get caught. I guess you were born unlucky."

42

BLAME SOCIETY TECHNIQUE

In this approach, the interrogator must be on the alert for an attitude of self-pity on the part of the subject, perhaps some comment referring to the breaks he never got or some event you've discovered in his background. It may have been the teacher who kept him after school and introduced him to his first sex act. It may have been the fellow who offered him a quarter and then practiced acts of perversion on him in the park. But at any rate, no matter what the case may be, we supply a built-in excuse for what the suspect did by blaming society or some other person for starting him on the road to ruin.

This technique is based on an innermost compulsion to confess that is present in all of us. You explain to the suspect that people give themselves away through physical and psychological manifestations of their guilt. We suggest that the change in his breathing rate, the flushing, and the sweating around his hairline and on his upper lip all come from the innermost compulsion to confess within him. You tell your subject that he actually wants to tell the truth but that there is just this one little thing that is holding him back. If you can help him over this big step, this first hump, you will. You tell him you know he wants to tell the truth because of that compulsion in all of us to confess our sins, perhaps supplying as encouragement the Catholic Church's prayer of confession: "I confess to almighty God ..."

43

COMPULSION TO CONFESS APPROACH

As an interrogator, you must bear in mind that often a person under the influence of liquor is no longer afraid of authority. He is no longer afraid of the uniform or the title of the detective, sergeant, or whatever your title may be. We can no longer depend on these demonstrations of authority to affect him. In fact, the uniform or title may do the exact opposite—the suspect may now become belligerent. When interrogating a drunk, you have to humor or flatter him, but be careful not to berate him.

44

DRUNK
TECHNIQUE

Care must be taken when interrogating females. If at all possible, have a policewoman right outside the door listening to the conversation. The policewoman is placed there for the protection of the interrogator to prevent the female subject from claiming she was taken advantage of.

45

INTERROGATION OF FEMALES

First, attempt to find out whether or not the woman you are questioning has any children. If she has a child, talk about that child. Ask about the age, the sex, and what school the child goes to. Ask whether she has any pictures. Praise the child, tell her how good-looking it is. Tell her it looks like her. Refer to her love for the child. Reiterate that her prime function in life is to reproduce. That is what God placed her on Earth for. It makes no difference whether or not the woman we are speaking to is a prostitute or an ordinary thief

employed by a bank. Women are generally emotional, and an emotional approach is best to use on them. We can use the emotions of love, jealously, and fear. We can appeal to her love for her parents and her children or to jealousy of her husband or boyfriend. Allude to how her husband will be enjoying himself if she goes to jail. Play upon her fear of jail—the cotton dresses that they wear in jail made out of jute cloth, the floppy shoes. Tell her she will no longer be seen as an individual; she will be classed as a unit. From there, it is easy to slide into the "Heaven and Hell Technique" described on page 31.

When speaking to a retarded person, we must keep our questions short and simple. Use the "K.I.S.S." (Keep It Simple, Stupid) method. In many instances we have to explain every question to our subject at a grade four or five level. We must be perfectly sure that he understands each question and that he understands the answer he is giving. Remember—explain, explain, explain in terms that are easily understandable.

46

RETARDED PERSON TECHNIQUE

When interviewing juveniles, it is important to keep the following points in mind:

47

TECHNIQUE FOR JUVENILES

- Do not be belligerent
- Try to understand the suspect's point of view
- Listen to the suspect
- Provide an excuse for what happened

With respect to the last point, you can use the child's parents, society, school, jealousy, recognition, or a mistake. Ask the child what he thinks is going to happen to him if he is found guilty. Amazingly, most juveniles believe that they will immediately go to jail if they confess. When you explain to them that they will not go to jail, that all they will do is appear in front of a juvenile judge or be spoken to by a social worker, they are very relieved. Use an example, perhaps explaining to them that last week there was a boy or a girl involved in the very same offense, and all that happened was that he or she was referred to the social agency for probation, nothing more.

There are several points to bear in mind when interrogating a car thief. The interrogator should always ask him what the mileage is, who he bought it from, what's in the glove compartment, what's in the trunk, and numerous other questions that only the owner of the car would know. You might also ask what type of oil he used and when he last had the car serviced.

In this technique, as in many others, the disposition of the interrogator is most important. An even disposition and an overall calmness will have a settling effect on some subjects and get them to talk. Other subjects are more susceptible to rapid-fire questions that do not give them any time to ponder the answers. Remember, never ask them to confess, simply ask for the truth.

48

CAR THIEF TECHNIQUE

It is most important not to apply this technique to a person who is psychotic. The psychopath does not have a conscience, as you and I know. But it can be used effectively on subjects who are of sound mind, and especially those who you have reason to believe are religious. Your approach may be something like this:

49

CONSCIENCE
TECHNIQUE

"John, it is quite possible you may beat us on this case, and I am going to tell you something. If you beat us, you beat yourself, because as long as you live, every day of your life you will see that little girl, you will hear her screams, you will wake up in the night screaming yourself. Will you be able to live with that, John? Will you be able to live with yourself? When you look at your own child will you see this other little child? Do you never think that maybe this urge could come over you and you could do the same thing to your own child? You will dream about the church. In your dreams you will hear that organ playing, John, and every note that that organ plays will hit your heart like a trip hammer. You will think of them placing that little girl's body down into the cold earth, and you will see the little statue, a little lamb, with the inscription underneath it. The Lamb of God on her grave. You will pray to God, John, every day of your life, you will pray that it didn't really happen. But it happened. And it is not too late to ask God for forgiveness, John."

50

FETISH TECHNIQUE

In many crimes today, the investigator runs across what might appear to be a fetish on the part of the criminal who committed the crime. Many times we refer to this as a "modus operandi." These fetishes may occur—and usually do occur—in sex crimes, for instance, when the breasts of the female victim are bitten or the private parts mutilated in some way. Perhaps hair has been removed from either the head or pubic areas. Or it may be that the victim's underclothing was removed. Whatever odd detail we discover at the scene of the crime, we must remember that it may prove very useful in questioning the suspect.

To use this technique effectively, the interrogator must delve into the background of the suspect by asking such questions as: "What do you remember most about your childhood? What was the best thing that happened to you? What was the worst thing that happened to you?" Questions pertaining to his relationship with his mother, father, brothers and sisters, teachers at school, or other people in the community in which he lives often shed some light on the way he was disciplined by parents or teachers or treated by the other children. This may give you a clue as to his particular fetish.

There are certainly countless interrogation techniques that have been employed and will be employed by police officers in the investigation of crimes of all sorts, but they all basically follow the same lines as the approaches detailed in this manual. There are as many techniques of interrogation as there are facets of human nature. If you are interested in becoming an effective interrogator, you must study human nature and be cognizant of those things that affect human nature. You must read avidly every article pertaining to the manipulation of human behavior.

As police officers, we must constantly remind ourselves that we are servants of the public, not its masters. Moreover, we must never overstep the boundaries of human dignity.

CONCLUSION